Simplified Classics

10 CLASSICAL FAVORITES FOR PIANO SOLO

Arranged by Glenda Austin

ISBN 978-1-4234-0796-6

WILLIS MUSIC

EXCLUSIVELY DISTRIBUTED BY

HAL•LEONARD®
CORPORATION

7777 W. BLUEMOUND RD. P.O. BOX 13819 MILWAUKEE, WI 53213

In Australia Contact:
Hal Leonard Australia Pty. Ltd.
4 Lentara Court
Cheltenham, Victoria, 3192 Australia
Email: ausadmin@halleonard.com

Visit Hal Leonard Online at
www.halleonard.com

Canon in D

Johann Pachelbel
1653–1706
Arranged by Glenda Austin

Peacefully

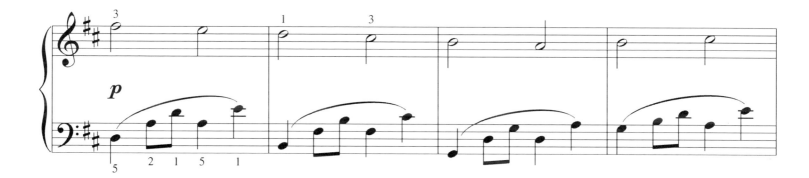

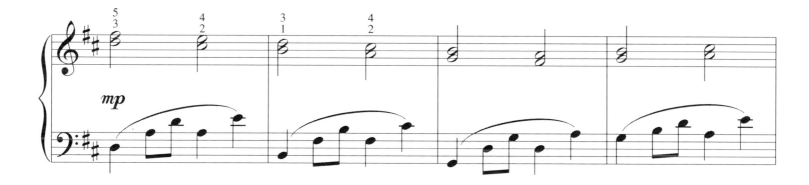

Jesu, Joy of Man's Desiring

from *Cantata BWV 147*

Johann Sebastian Bach
1685–1750
Arranged by Glenda Austin

Moderate and flowing

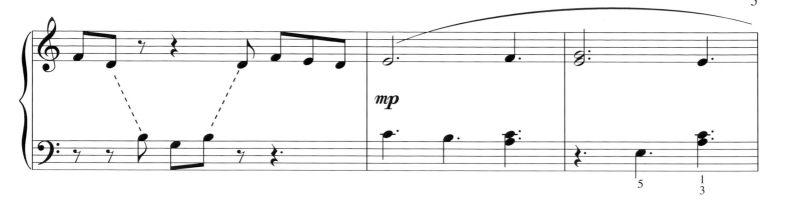

Spring

from *The Four Seasons*

Antonio Vivaldi
1678–1741
Arranged by Glenda Austin

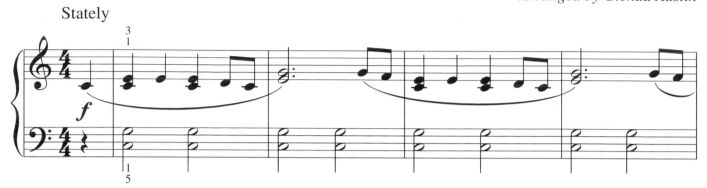

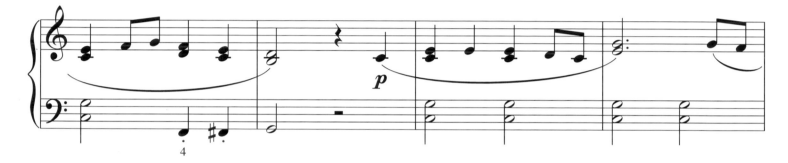

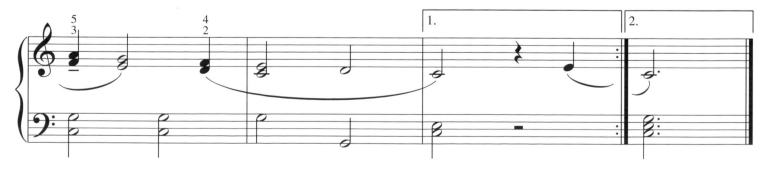

Funeral March of a Marionette

Charles Gounod
1818–1893
Arranged by Glenda Austin

Not too fast

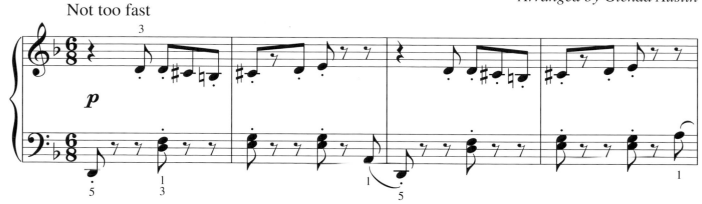

Polovtsian Dance No. 2

from *Prince Igor*

Alexander Borodin
1833–1887
Arranged by Glenda Austin

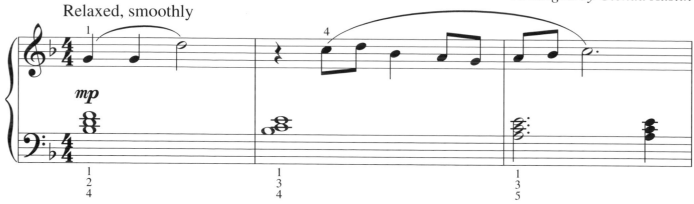

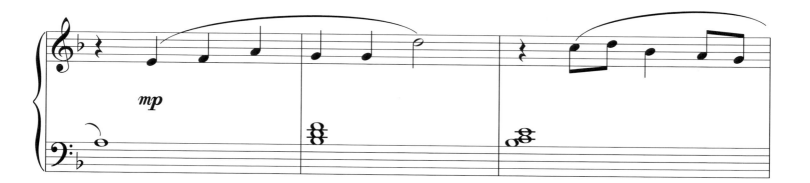

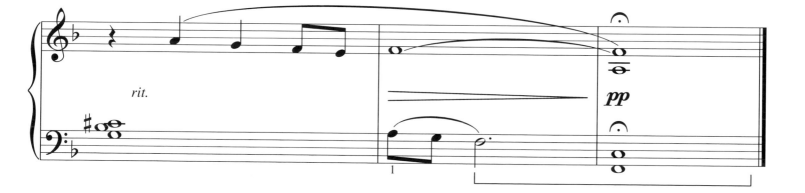

Dance of the Hours

from *La Gioconda*

Amilcare Ponchielli
1834–1886
Arranged by Glenda Austin

Lightly and not too fast

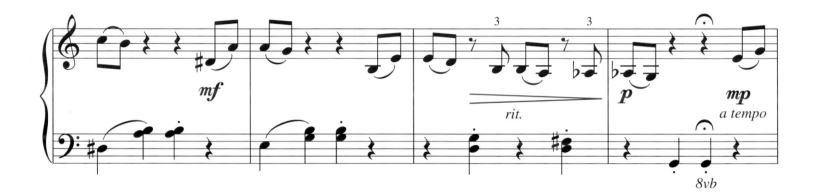

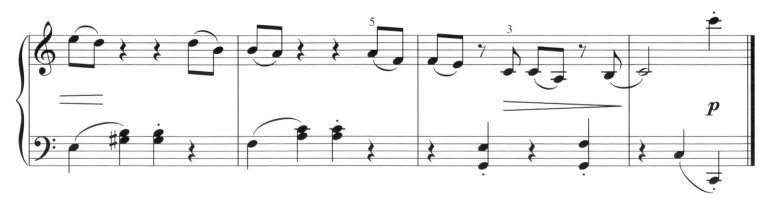

Toreador Song

from *Carmen*

Georges Bizet
1838–1875
Arranged by Glenda Austin

With spirit

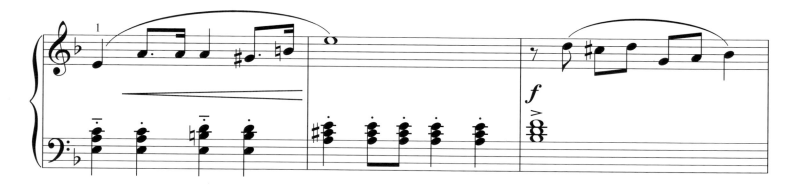

Hungarian Dance No. 5

Johannes Brahms
1833–1897
Arranged by Glenda Austin

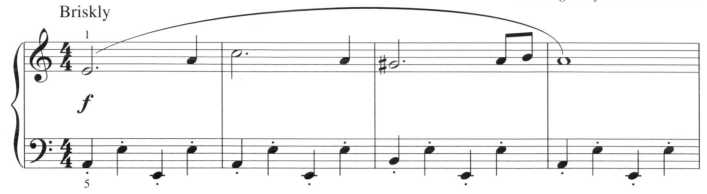

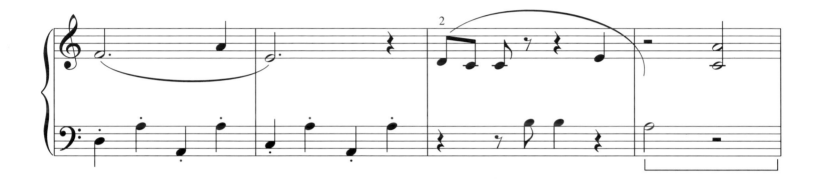

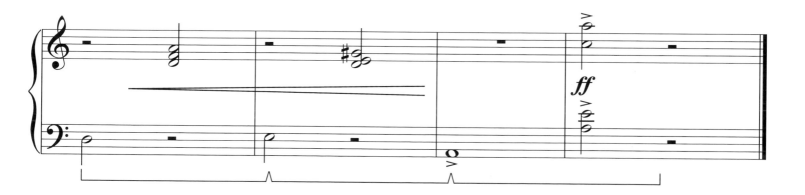

Blue Danube Waltz

Johann Strauss
1825–1899
Arranged by Glenda Austin

Moderato, with a lilt

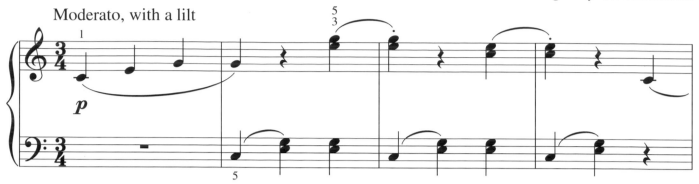

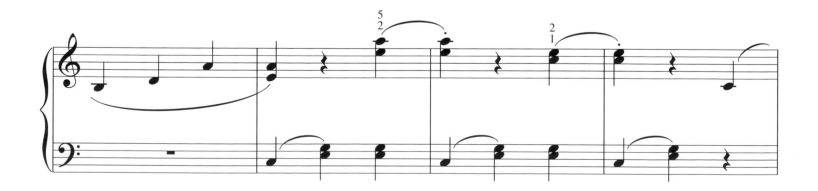

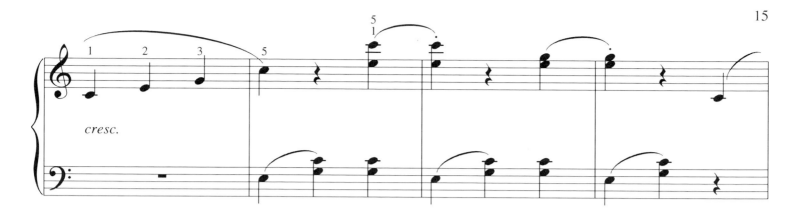

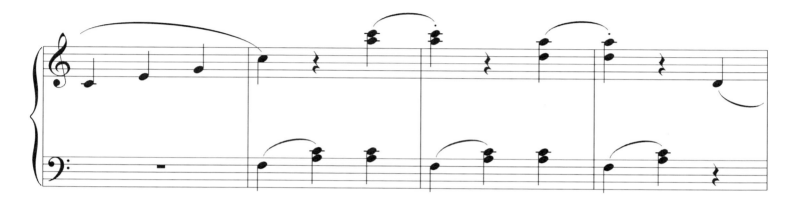

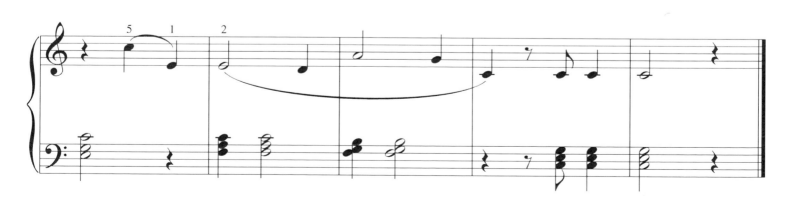

Minuet in G

Ignacy Jan Paderewski
1860–1941
Arranged by Glenda Austin

Stately

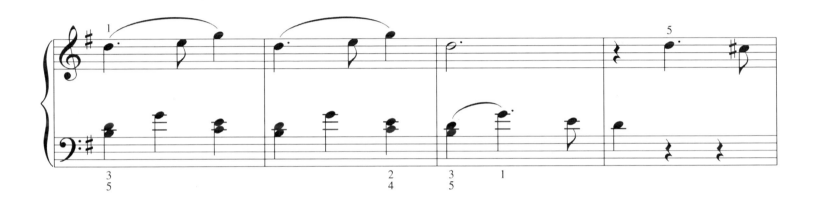

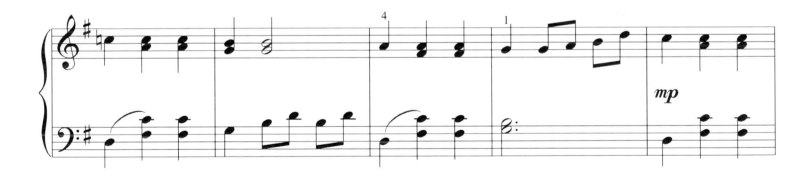

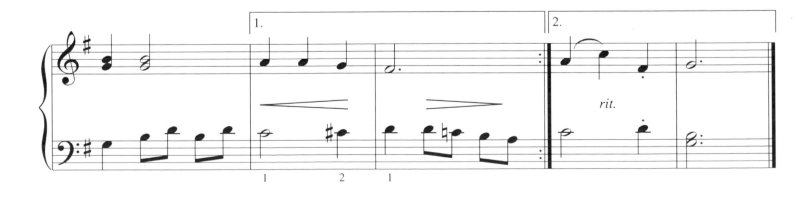